A long long time ago, in the village of Drumnadrochit, in a little white cottage near Urquhart Castle on the shores of Loch Ness, lived a little girl called Dorit. Her real name was Dorothy but everyone called her Drumnadrochit Dorit because it was fun to say and Dorit liked it.

There were no other boys and girls living near so Drumnadrochit Dorit spent a lot of time on her own playing by the lochside. She used to long for a friend to play with. One day she was running down to the loch as usual when suddenly she noticed a big ripple of water. Then an enormous head popped out of the middle of the pool.

'Brr! The water's cold today,' said the head.

Being a very brave little girl Dorit was not at all afraid. She looked calmly at the head and said, 'Who are you?'

'I'm Nessie, the Loch Ness Monster and I'm cold and lonely. Who are you?'

'Don't be silly!' said Dorit. 'There are no such things as monsters, I don't believe you!'

The monster glared at her. 'I've been here for hundreds of years, everyone knows about me. If you want to know if I'm real touch my head.' She bent her head down and Dorit reached out and gently touched her skin. If felt clean and very silky.
'I'm sorry I didn't believe you,' she said, 'but no one has ever told me about you.'
'That's because they're all frightened of me and that's why I'm lonely.'
'Well, I'm lonely too,' said Drumnadrochit Dorit. 'Shall we be friends?'
And she sat on a rock and they talked and talked until it was nearly dark and Dorit had to go home for tea but she promised to come back the next day.

Back at the little cottage, while she was having her tea, Dorit asked her Mummy and Daddy if they knew about the monster in the loch.

'There have been a lot of rumours about it for many many years,' said her father, 'but nobody will actually admit to having seen one. It's a pity, because if there really was a monster lots of tourists would come to the village and it would mean more jobs for people looking after the visitors.'

That night, when she went to bed, Dorit suddenly had a brilliant idea. She decided to go and see Nessie first thing the next morning.

A few days later a group of important people came to Drumnadrochit to celebrate the anniversary of the opening of the Caledonian Canal. As they walked down to the lochside Dorit went up to them and asked, 'Would you like to see the Loch Ness monster?'
They smiled and said 'Yes' but she could tell they didn't believe her.
'Follow me,' she said and she set off to the deep pool.

As they reached the shore Nessie heard the sounds of their footsteps so she knew they were coming. Slowly she rose out of the water, put her flippers on the bank and gave a great big smile of welcome.
Everyone was absolutely terrified! They screamed and shouted and turned and ran in all directions, scrambling to get away from the monster.

Poor Nessie was so upset! She didn't understand why they had all been frightened of her and she burst into tears. Dorit tried to console her but she was crying too. Nessie cried all the way down to the bottom of the loch and Dorit cried all the way home, but when she reached the cottage her Mummy and Daddy were laughing and laughing - they said it was the funniest thing they had ever seen.

Drumnadrochit Dorit thought her idea had been a failure but the next day the story was in all the papers and after that people came in buses, cars and trains from all over the world, just to see Nessie. There were lots of jobs for all the villagers and everyone was very happy, especially Nessie.